W9-AHH-594

Beni's Family Treasury

Stories for the Jewish Holidays

JANE BRESKIN ZALBEN

Henry Holt and Company · New York

The author wishes to thank Marc Chesire, who did the first book,
Brenda Bowen, whose inspiration began a series, and
Christy Ottaviano, who has continued to usher it on—with appreciation.

Henry Holt and Company, Inc., *Publishers since 1866*
115 West 18th Street, New York, New York 10011
Henry Holt is a registered trademark of Henry Holt and Company, Inc.

Published in Canada by Fitzhenry & Whiteside Ltd.,
195 Allstate Parkway, Markham, Ontario L3R 4T8

Library of Cataloging-in-Publication Data
Zalben, Jane Breskin.
Beni's family treasury: stories for the Jewish holidays / by Jane Breskin Zalben.
Contents: Happy New Year, Beni—Leo and Blossom's sukkah—Beni's first Chanukah—
Goldie's Purim—Happy Passover, Rosie. Summary: A collection of episodes
in the lives of Beni and his family shows them observing their Jewish traditions as
they celebrate the holidays of Rosh Hashanah, Sukkot, Chanukah, Purim, and Passover.
1. Jews—Juvenile fiction. [1. Jews—Fiction. 2. Holidays—Fiction.] I. Title.
PZ7.Z254Bc 1998 [E]—dc21 97-50303
ISBN 0-8050-5889-3/First Edition—1998
The artist used watercolor on opaline parchment to create the illustrations for this book.
Printed in Italy
1 3 5 7 9 10 8 6 4 2

To my family, with love

Since 1987, Jane Breskin Zalben has been creating wonderful stories about Beni and Sara and their colorful bear family. Her books have been praised for their warmth and humor, for their beautiful detail and craftsmanship, and for offering a window into the Jewish culture by way of holiday tradition. The Beni series continues to enjoy readership from children around the world. In fact, Ms. Zalben recently flew to Ethiopia and spoke with rural schoolchildren about her books. In 1996, Ms. Zalben wrote and illustrated *Beni's Family Cookbook for the Jewish Holidays*. This inventive cookbook blends storytelling with holiday recipes in an accessible, illustrated format for children and parents alike.

Jane Breskin Zalben was born in Queens, New York, and lives on Long Island with her family. She is a writer, a painter, a mother, a renowned cook—someone who is able to combine all of these talents with delicacy and charm when creating books for children. *Beni's Family Treasury: Stories for the Jewish Holidays* offers young readers a stellar collection of five of the best-known and best-loved Beni classics, all to be cherished between two covers.

CONTENTS

This book belongs to:

_____

Happy New Year, Beni

When Beni and Sara came home from school, they found a letter waiting for them.

Darlings,

Grandpa and I would like you to come for the holidays. We've set up the bedrooms. There's plenty of room. Everyone will be here.

Love and Kisses,

Grandma and Grandpa

"Does 'everyone' also mean cousin Max?" Beni asked. "Everyone means the whole family," Mama replied. Beni and Sara groaned. "We're going," Mama said.

So that week, Beni and Sara colored cards for
cousins Rosie, Max, Goldie, Molly, Sam, and
their friends Leo and Blossom down the street.
The morning before *Rosh Hashanah,* Papa packed up

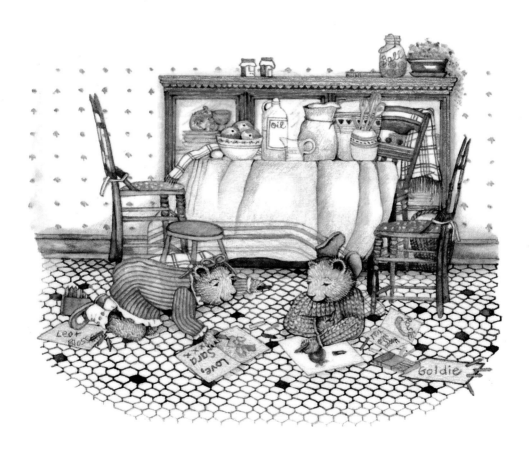

the car while Mama wrapped the special cakes and cookies Beni and Sara had baked with their parents the whole week long. *Rugelach. Mandlebrot. Strudel.* Before sundown, they got to Grandma and Grandpa's.

"Beni, darling," shouted Grandma.
"Sara, sweetheart," cried Grandpa.
Then the relatives started coming,
one by one, hugging and kissing each other.

Cousin Max tapped Sara on the shoulder.
He shot a rubber band at her, ran away, and
hid until she lit the candles with Grandma.

Grandpa lifted his wine cup and said the *Kiddush*.
Beni also said the prayer over a round raisin
challah. Max started giggling. Beni kicked him
under the table. Grandpa ripped the challah.
Everyone dipped pieces of sliced apples and challah
into honey. "To a sweet, good year! *L'shanah Tovah!*"
Papa cheered. "Let it be a happy and healthy one!"

Grandma passed fresh figs and plump dates around the table. Max stuffed the last dates into his mouth before Beni could eat any. His cheeks were all full and puffed out. Beni made a face. Mama turned to Beni. "Stop it! Save room for dinner," she said. "What did *I* do?" Beni asked, feeling angry inside.

That night, when the cousins were getting ready
for bed, Max put wet plastic spiders and slimy
worms under everyone's pillows. "Now you've gone
and done it! Hippopotamus breath!" Beni screamed.
The parents yelled, "Go to sleep. That's enough!"
Beni wondered, What about a happy new year?

The next morning, everyone walked to the *synagogue*.
Beni's grandparents greeted friends when they got inside.
Beni picked up the *Maḥzor,* a special prayer book,
and read along. Papa blew the *shofar* like a musical
instrument. It made loud, long, sharp sounds. Sara
covered her ears, while the little cousins jumped in
their seats to see where the noise was coming from.

"What's that?" Cousin Rosie asked, pointing
to the front of the synagogue. Grandpa explained,
"It's a ram's horn announcing the holiday and the
beginning of a new year. Rosh Hashanah
means 'Head of the Year.'"
The *rabbi* talked about Rosh Hashanah.
"These are the *'Days of Awe.'* We look back
at all the things we've done in the past year."
Beni looked at Max. Max stared at Beni,
while the *cantor* chanted beautiful songs and
the congregation sang.

In the late afternoon, Grandpa asked Beni, Max,
and all the cousins to walk together to a brook.
Many of Grandma and Grandpa's friends were there,
saying prayers and throwing bits of bread into
the water. "What are they doing?" Beni asked.
Grandpa leaned toward Beni. "This is called *Tashlikh*."
Grandpa threw a tiny piece of bread into the brook.
"We get rid of what we did during the year that
wasn't so nice and we begin with a new, clean slate.
Would you like a piece?" Beni remembered his mistakes.
He took a small crust of bread from the palm of Grandpa's
hand, tossed it into the brook, and watched it go downstream.

"This is for teasing Sara all the time."
Sara took a piece. "This is for teasing Beni."
Beni took another piece, and gave Max half.
Max ate it and laughed. Beni continued,
"And this is for kicking Max under the
table yesterday." Max bowed his head,
and threw some crumbs into the brook.
"All right, already. I'm sorry, Beni, for
hogging all the dates and figs."
"Me too, Max. I'm also sorry."

Grandpa hugged them both, tightly.

Beni looked up at his grandfather.

"Next year, I'll try to be even better."

Grandpa looked at Beni and whispered,

"Just be you. Happy New Year, Beni."

Max pulled at Grandpa. "I can almost
smell Grandma's noodle pudding."
Beni thought of his grandma's *kugel* as
they ran across the bridge toward home.
When they got back, Max kissed Beni.

"Yuck!" yelled Beni, wiping the kiss off his cheek.
"Guess I have something to add to next year!" Max cried.
"No you don't!" shouted Beni. And he kissed Max back.
"Yuck!" yelled Max. And they both fell on a bed of leaves,
laughing.

TANTE ROSE'S
ROUND RAISIN CHALLAH

2 packages of dry yeast	2 tablespoons vegetable oil
pinch of sugar	2/3 cup honey
3 large eggs	8 cups flour
1 egg white	1/2 cup raisins
1 teaspoon of salt	1/2 tablespoon cinnamon

1. Dissolve yeast in 2 cups warm water, around 105°–115°. Add sugar. Stir. Set aside for 10 minutes at room temperature until the liquid foams.
2. Beat 3 eggs and 1 egg white. (Reserve yolk.) Add salt, oil, and honey to this mixture, continuing to beat.
3. Put flour in large bowl. Indent center. Gradually add yeast mixture to flour, stirring center with a wooden spoon until it is absorbed. Stir in liquid from Step 2.
4. Now mix by hand. Fold in raisins and cinnamon. Sprinkle lightly with flour if the dough is sticky. When dough is smooth, place in greased bowl. Cover bowl with dish towel. Keep in warm place for 1–2 hours. Let dough rise until double in size. Punch down.

5. Knead dough for about 5 minutes on a floured board or surface until the dough tightens and is not sticky. Divide into 3 balls. Form each ball and roll into a snakelike rope about 18″ long. Shape circle by twisting the rope into a spiral with the end at the top of the center.
6. Let it rise again uncovered for 1 hour on greased pan or cookie sheet until doubled in size.
7. Preheat oven to 375°.
8. Brush loaves with mixture of beaten egg yolk and 1 teaspoon cold water to make a glaze on challah.
9. Bake for 20–25 minutes or until golden brown.

Makes 3 loaves.

The *round challah,* traditional on this holiday, symbolizes the cycle of life and its seasons. It is also said to be like a ladder to heaven. The bread is more special for its shape than the weekly braided Friday-night Shabbat challah, and it is dipped into honey instead of salt so the new year is sweet and filled with joy.

Leo & Blossom's Sukkah

*L*eo and Blossom went outside to play.
They saw Papa taking sticks and tools
from the shed. Blossom asked,
"Papa, what are you doing?"
"*Sukkot* is coming soon," he said.
"I'm going to build the *sukkah.*"
Leo turned to his sister, "Let's build our
own sukkah right next to Mama and Papa's."

Leo made a roof from leaves and pine boughs.
Blossom wove willows between the branches.
Beni came by and asked, "Can I help?" He
hung many different fruits and vegetables.

Sara strung popcorn and cranberries.
Rosie made long colorful paper chains.
And their friend Max wondered aloud,
"Do you think there's too much hanging?"
But everyone was too busy to listen.

Outside the air was crisp.
Inside it smelled sweet,
like hay in a barn.
They were safe, warm, and dry.
When no one was looking,
Leo pulled an apple off a stem.

Suddenly an orange bounced on
Leo's head. Then a pear onto Beni's.
Peppers tumbled, hitting Rosie and Max.
Grapes and lemons began to roll.

Sara slipped into Blossom, who fell
as a tomato splattered on her new dress.
She began to cry. "Look at our sukkah."
Leo nudged Blossom. "We'll begin again."

But this time their parents helped.

Later that night they had a large feast.
Everyone ate and sang. Papa told a story
about how the Jews fled Egypt and lived
in huts for forty years in the desert,
and how there was a big harvest festival
when they settled in the Land of Israel.
Blossom said, "Just like when the Pilgrims
came to America and celebrated Thanksgiving."
Papa said, "Thanksgiving is like Sukkot.
We give thanks for the first crop.
It is the holiday to ask for rain."
"Rain means life," Mama added.

Drops of water started to fall through
the twigs and leaves. Everyone looked up.
Then, outside, they heard Leo's laugh.
Mama peeked around the corner.

"Leo, get in here and shut off that hose!"
Blossom laughed. And so did all their friends,
including Mama and Papa, as they dried Leo off.

"Could we do this again next year?" Blossom asked.
Mama and Papa nodded yes. Leo smiled and said,
"Next year we'll build the sukkah even better!"
"How?" asked Blossom. "It's beautiful now."

"We'll hang pumpkins and watermelons!"
Mama and Papa just looked at Leo and sighed.
"Okay, Indian corn and squash," Leo said.
"To next year!" Everyone chimed in.

The moonlight cast shadows in the stillness.
Stars twinkled between the boughs above.
As the family fell asleep, they heard the
gentle pitter-patter of rain.

SUKKOT

Sukkot is the Festival of Booths, or Tabernacles. It is a joyous festival that commemorates the final gathering of the harvest. At Sukkot a temporary hut (or booth) is built. In it a family eats, drinks, and sleeps during the holiday, and is reminded of how the Israelites lived in the wilderness. The hut may have three sides or four, with walls of bamboo poles or canvas, and a loose roof of tree branches of evergreens or palms. The covering of branches should be heavy enough for there to be shade during the day, but open enough for the stars to be seen at night.

In her right hand, on page 41, Blossom carries a *lulav* (or palm branch) attached to two willow boughs and three myrtle branches; in her left hand she carries an *etrog* (or citrus fruit). These are the four festival symbols, called the Four Species: palm, willow, myrtle, and citron. The waving of the *lulav* in different directions symbolizes that God is everywhere.

In 1620, when the Pilgrims came to America, they held a harvest festival. They based their first Thanksgiving on the ancient holiday of Sukkot.

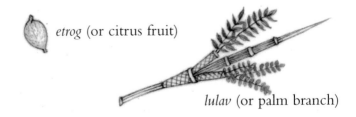

etrog (or citrus fruit)

lulav (or palm branch)

THE SUKKAH

FRUITS AND VEGETABLES YOU CAN HANG IN THE SUKKAH

The Seven Major Fruits of Israel are:

wheat

olives

barley

dates

grapes

figs

pomegranates

Leo and Blossom and their friends also hung or brought in:

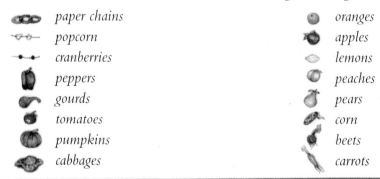

paper chains

oranges

popcorn

apples

cranberries

lemons

peppers

peaches

gourds

pears

tomatoes

corn

pumpkins

beets

cabbages

carrots

Beni's First Chanukah

 The morning air was cold.
Beni sank deeper under the quilt,
and curled his paws with excitement.
At sunset, it would be the first night of *Chanukah,* the
first Chanukah Beni would be old enough to remember.

After breakfast, Beni helped Mama peel potatoes for *latkes*.

His sister, Sara, made applesauce for the pancakes.

The kitchen smelled of fresh cinnamon and lemon rind.

Sara spooned sour cream into Mama's best bowl
and Beni helped Papa fry jelly doughnuts.
Sugar powdered their noses.

The rest of the morning, Beni and Sara
searched for their Chanukah presents,

one for each of the eight nights,
but they found nothing.

Light flakes of snow began to dust the trees.
Beni and Sara pressed their noses against the
windowpanes, hoping they could play in the flurry.
Mama said, "Dress warmly."
Papa wrapped them in long woolen scarves.

Sara tried to make snowballs, but they fell apart.
Beni laughed. "They look like Mama's potato pancakes!"
And they pretended to eat them.

"Let's visit Sasha and Christopher," Beni said.
Sara followed him down the hill, finding treasures
along the way. And so did Beni.

When they got to their friends' house, Beni placed
a special pinecone on the lower bough of Sasha and
Christopher's tree. Sara reached as high as she could,
and nestled some red winter berries in a branch above.
They all made a star out of twigs and put it on the top
of the tree. The pink-and-orange sky glowed on a mound
of snow. Beni and Sara returned home, inviting Sasha and
Christopher to their house.

When nighttime came, the whole family arrived—
grandparents, aunts, uncles, and cousins.
Beni emptied a box of colored candles.
Beni chose his favorite color,
yellow, and green for the *shammash*.
Papa picked up Beni in his arms,
and held the bright green candle.
Beni repeated the prayer after Papa.
Mama smiled proudly.

The light from the *menorah* warmed
the frosted sill outside. Beni and Sara
taught Sasha and Christopher how to
spin the *dreidel*. Everybody sang songs.
Then it was time for the gifts.

Sara got hers first. Then she helped her
little brother and cousins unwrap their presents.
Beni got just what he wanted.
Sasha and Christopher each untied a bag
of chocolate gold coins.

Everyone sat around the fire.
Grandpa told the story of Chanukah, about
how the oil burned magically for eight nights.
Beni pretended to be a *Maccabee* warrior.

As the first night of Chanukah came to an end,
Sasha and Christopher said, "It was wonderful."
Beni asked his parents, "Could they come the
second night too?" Mama and Papa nodded yes.

At bedtime, Beni's parents kissed him good night
and said, "Happy Chanukah!"
Beni held his new stuffed bear a little tighter.
"This was my best Chanukah ever."
Sara tiptoed in. Mama and Papa hugged Beni
and whispered, "It was ours too."

MAMA'S LATKES

4–5 large potatoes
1 medium onion
2 large eggs

1/4 cup matzoh meal
salt and pepper
vegetable oil

1. Peel potatoes, wash in cold water, grate finely.
2. Grate onion on larger side of grater.
3. Beat 2 eggs and add to mixture.
4. Blend in matzoh meal, and salt and pepper to taste with other ingredients.
5. Heat 1" layer of vegetable oil in large frying pan. Drop in 1 heaping tablespoon of mixture for each latke, and when it sizzles turn over until it's crisp and golden.
6. Drain on paper towels.
7. Serve with sour cream or applesauce.

Serves about 6, depending on their appetites!
Beni eats 4 pancakes. He loves Mama's latkes.

מגלת
אסתר
המלכה
ומרדכי
היהודי

The Scroll of Esther the Queen
and Mordecai the Jew

Goldie's Purim

*G*ood smells of *hamantaschen* baking filled every corner of the house. Mama and Papa cut the flat pastry into circles, spreading poppy seeds, thick prune butter, and sweet apricot preserves in each center. Goldie, her sister, Molly, and her brother, Sam, sewed their costumes for the *Purim* play the following day.

They practiced their lines while they went
around the neighborhood giving *shalach manot*—
little gifts of food—to their family and friends.

At bedtime Goldie put the finishing touches
on her dress. She laid her crown and veil on the
rocker. Mama gave her a big good-night hug.
"You'll be wonderful tomorrow as Esther."
Goldie closed her eyes, dreaming of her
special part.

The next morning every seat in the synagogue
was filled. Goldie saw her grandparents, aunts,
uncles, and little cousins. Her best friends, Leo
and Blossom, waved.

Goldie was too scared to wave back.

First Goldie heard her sister, Molly,
who was the beautiful Queen Vashti.
"Even though the king has called
for me, I will not go and see him!"

Then Goldie heard her cousin Beni,
who played King Ahasuerus.
"Vashti is no longer the Queen!
Search the kingdom for a new wife."

Sam, who had the part of Mordecai, said,
"I will bring my cousin Esther to the palace."
Now Goldie knew it was her turn. Everyone
looked at Goldie. Her legs trembled. She
didn't move. She didn't speak. Sam shouted,

"Go, Esther!" Goldie thought about how brave Esther was, and how she'd have to be brave too. Goldie stepped forward and said all her lines perfectly. At the end of the play, the longest and loudest applause was for Goldie.

Then Papa took out the *Megillah*. He opened the
scroll and read the story of Esther, who became
Queen of Persia and saved the Jewish people
from wicked Haman. Every time the name of
Haman was spoken, the children whirled their
groggers in the air and stamped their feet,
making a lot of noise.

They paraded around the temple in their
costumes with all the parents, danced and sang,
saw a puppet show, and ate a special dinner.

Everybody ate the hamantaschen that Goldie's
family had baked. Poppy seeds got stuck
between their teeth.

That night Goldie looked outside her
bedroom window at the winter moon.
The last patches of snow had already
begun to melt. Spring was on its way.
Goldie heard Sam snoring in his room,
rumbling like a grogger. She giggled.
Mama tiptoed in. "I'm very proud of you."
Goldie looked up. "I was scared, Mama."
"But you stopped being scared. Every person
can be brave if she tries." And she kissed Goldie.
"Like Esther was with the King!" said Goldie.
Then she smiled. "And like I was today."

PURIM PLAY (Spiel)

Cast of Characters

King Ahasuerus (*Beni*)	Ruler of the vast Persian Empire.
Queen Vashti (*Molly*)	Favorite wife of King Ahasuerus until he banished her for disobeying his commands.
Esther (*Goldie*)	A beautiful young Jewish woman chosen by Ahasuerus to be his new Queen. Through the bravery of Esther the Jewish people were saved.
Mordecai (*Sam*)	Esther's cousin, who warned the King of a plot against his life by Bigthan and Teresh, members of the court. He became a trusted advisor to Ahasuerus after Haman's death.
Haman (*Max*)	The chief advisor to King Ahasuerus. Haman hated Mordecai because Mordecai refused to bow down to him. Haman cast lots (*purim*) to determine the day on which the Jewish people would be destroyed. Haman's evil plot to kill all the Jews of Persia was stopped when Esther told the King of Haman's plan.

Hamantaschen, named after the wicked Haman, are triangle-shaped pastries eaten on the joyful holiday of Purim. Some people think that Haman wore a three-cornered hat. Others say that he had pointy ears that looked like triangles. These pastries are also known as "Haman's pockets" because in Yiddish *tashn* means "pockets." Hamantaschen, along with fruits and nuts, are given out in gift packages (shalach manot) to friends, as Mordecai instructed all Jews to do on the first Purim celebration.

HAMANTASCHEN

3 cups flour
1/2 tsp. baking soda
2 tsps. baking powder
1/4 tsp. salt
2/3 cup sugar
1/8 tsp. cinnamon

1/4 cup cream cheese
1/2 cup margarine
1/2 tsp. vanilla
2 tbsps. milk
2 tbsps. orange juice
1 egg

filling (see below)

1. Sift flour, baking soda, and baking powder.
2. Then mix in salt, sugar, and cinnamon. Set aside.
3. Cream together softened cream cheese and margarine. Add vanilla, milk, orange juice, and egg to creamed mixture, blend well.
4. To form a soft dough, add dry ingredients to creamed ingredients in a food processor or mixer.
5. Place dough onto a lightly floured board or table and roll out with rolling pin until dough is about 1/8" thick.
6. Cut into 2" circles using an upside-down glass.
7. Fill each circle with 1/2 tsp. of filling, which can be poppy seeds, prune or apple butter, apricot preserves, pitted cherries, chocolate chips, or minced walnuts and honey.
8. Press three sides of the circle together and pinch to make triangles. Place hamantaschen on a greased cookie sheet.
9. Bake 10 minutes or until golden brown in a preheated 350° oven.

Note: This is a dairy recipe. If pareve, substitute water for milk, and additional margarine for cream cheese.

Happy Passover,
Rosie

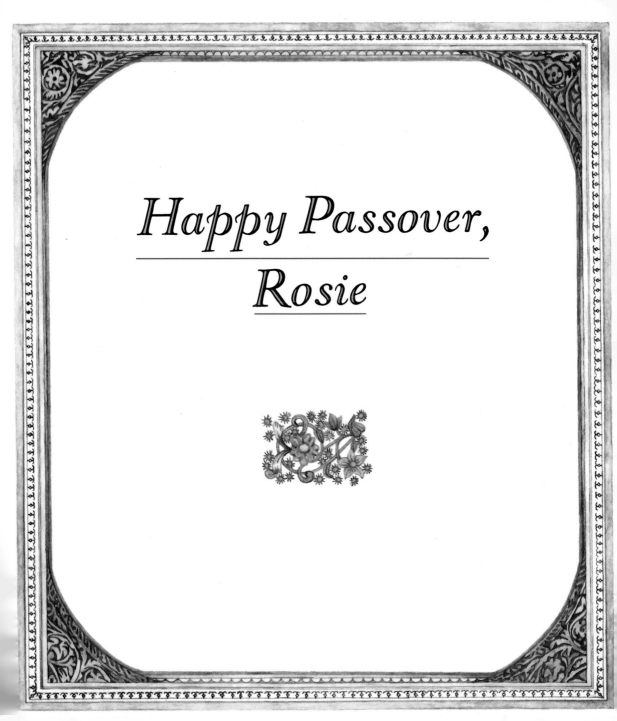

*T*he night before the first *Passover Seder,* Rosie
and her brother Max hunted for stray bread crumbs
with wooden spoons. Grandma dusted the shelves
with a feather while Grandpa held a glowing candle
and a small box for the crumbs.

The next morning birds were chirping when
Rosie opened her eyes. The air felt like spring.
Rosie and Max helped Grandpa burn the box of
chametz while Grandma stirred the soup she was
making for the Seder meal. She sighed, "Mmm.
These *matzoh balls* are light and fluffy." Max
whispered, "Remember last year when Papa
made them and they were like bowling balls?"
Rosie giggled, and watched them float.

Before sundown family and friends arrived.
Aunt Gertie gave Rosie a huge wet kiss on
the cheek, and Uncle Hymie nearly crushed
her with his big hug.

When it was time for the Seder, Rosie sat
next to her cousin Beni. Grandpa picked up
the three matzohs in the blue-velvet pouch
embroidered with gold thread. He broke
the middle *matzoh*, the *afikoman*, in half
and wrapped it in a cloth. When no one was
looking, he hid the matzoh. Rosie wondered,
Where? And when? She thought she had been
watching Grandpa the whole time.

Then it was time to ask the Four Questions. Rosie was the youngest, so she was supposed to ask them all by herself. She had been practicing with Max for weeks. Rosie looked at the faces

around the table. Mama smiled as Rosie began.
"Why is this night different from all other nights?
On all other nights we eat bread or matzoh:
Why tonight only matzoh?" Papa smiled also.

Max helped a little with the second question.
Sara whispered the next one when Rosie forgot
a word. Rosie and Beni said the last question
together. Mama and Papa were very, very proud.
Everyone said the *Ten Plagues* and sang "*Dayenu.*"

While Grandpa recited the *Haggadah*, Rosie
spent most of her time under the table,
crawling between her aunts' and uncles' legs.
She peeked out when it was time for the
bitter herbs, the *ḥaroset*, and finally the meal.

The family was so stuffed, nobody could move
an inch—except Rosie and Max and their cousins,
who ran around searching for the hidden matzoh.
Rosie looked under the pillow on Grandpa's chair.
"I found the afikoman!" she cried. Grandpa took

Rosie aside and gave her a shiny silver coin.
And he winked. Rosie gave Grandpa a big smile.
Then he poured a glass of wine for the prophet
Elijah and left it in front of an empty chair.
Rosie and Max played with Beni and Sara.

Suddenly there was a loud knock at the front door. Grandma opened it. Outside was very dark. "Is it the ghost of Elijah?" asked Uncle Hymie. Rosie trembled. Uncle Hymie began to chuckle. Then Aunt Gertie. Then Mama and Papa, and all the cousins. From beneath a coat came Grandpa. The relatives laughed very loudly. Rosie didn't laugh at all. She wouldn't go near Grandpa for a long time.

Grandpa came over to Rosie when he saw she was feeling better. "Sweetheart, I'm sorry I scared you. See, it's me, Grandpa. I'll always be your *Zaide*. Forever." And he touched his hand to Rosie's. "Can I give you your special gift now?" Rosie nodded.

Grandpa gave her a kiss. A hug. And her own Haggadah.
Rosie hugged her Grandpa. "Happy Passover, Rosie."
"Happy Passover, Grandpa." Grandma came over
and hugged Rosie also. "And Grandma too."
Her apron still smelled of chicken soup.

THE SEDER PLATE

1. Egg (*beitzah*): A roasted egg symbolizes the festival offering in the Temple and the mourning of the destruction of the Temple. But the egg can also be thought of as a symbol of fertility and renewal.

2. Shank bone (*zeroa*): A scorched portion of the leg bone of a lamb represents the *paschal* offering, in memory of the ancient Temple sacrifice.

3. Bitter herbs (*maror*): Sometimes romaine lettuce, sometime horseradish, this recalls the bitterness of slavery in Egypt.

4. *Haroset*: This sweet paste of chopped apples, nuts, and cinnamon mixed with a little wine represents the mortar used by the Israelites while they labored in bondage to the Pharaohs. *Haroset* tempers the bitterness of the maror. A strip of cinnamon bark may be placed near the *haroset* to represent the strawless clay bricks that the Israelites were forced to make in Egypt.

5. Parsley (*karpas*): A sprig of parsley represents spring, life, and hope. Dipped in salt water, the *karpas* suggests the bitterness of salty tears.

6. Grated horseradish (*hazaret*): This additional bitter herb is eaten with the *haroset* in a matzoh sandwich (*korekh*) to show life has two sides—the bitter and the sweet.

7. Matzoh: Three matzohs placed in the center of the Seder plate stand for the unity of the three tribes: Cohen, Levi, and Israel. (The matzohs may be put on a separate plate.) The matzoh itself is unleavened bread. It stands for the bread that was baking and didn't have time to rise when the Jews made their Exodus from Egypt.

THE FOUR QUESTIONS

The youngest child present asks:

Why is this night different from all other nights?

1. On all other nights we eat bread or matzoh:
Why tonight only matzoh?

2. On all other nights we eat any kind of herb:
Why tonight only bitter herbs?

3. On all other nights we don't dip the herbs even once:
Why tonight do we dip twice?

4. On all other nights we eat either sitting or reclining:
Why tonight do we all recline?

מַה נִּשְׁתַּנָּה הַלַּיְלָה הַזֶּה מִכָּל־הַלֵּילוֹת.

1 שֶׁבְּכָל־הַלֵּילוֹת אָנוּ אוֹכְלִין חָמֵץ וּמַצָּה. הַלַּיְלָה הַזֶּה
כֻּלּוֹ מַצָּה:

2 שֶׁבְּכָל־הַלֵּילוֹת אָנוּ אוֹכְלִין שְׁאָר יְרָקוֹת. הַלַּיְלָה הַזֶּה
מָרוֹר:

3 שֶׁבְּכָל־הַלֵּילוֹת אֵין אָנוּ מַטְבִּילִין אֲפִלּוּ פַּעַם אֶחָת.
הַלַּיְלָה הַזֶּה שְׁתֵּי פְעָמִים:

4 שֶׁבְּכָל־הַלֵּילוֹת אָנוּ אוֹכְלִין בֵּין יוֹשְׁבִין וּבֵין מְסֻבִּין.
הַלַּיְלָה הַזֶּה כֻּלָּנוּ מְסֻבִּין:

GLOSSARY

Afikoman (A-fee-KO-mun): the middle matzoh of three, half of which is hidden, and later eaten for dessert during the Passover Seder.

Cantor (CAN-tor): the leader of the synagogue congregation in song.

Challah (CHA-lah, with the guttural *ch* of the Scottish *loch*): an egg-enriched bread served at a Shabbat meal.

Chametz (CHA-mets): Hebrew for leaven-fermented dough. Anything not kosher for Passover (bread, grain, cereal, etc).

Chanukah (CHA-noo-ka): eight-day "Festival of Lights" celebrating the victory of the Maccabee warriors over Antiochus, who tried to make the Jews believe in many gods instead of One God. (Usually falls around December.)

Dayenu (Di-YAY-noo): Hebrew for "it would be enough."

Days of Awe: Rosh Hashanah and Yom Kippur.

Dreidel (DRAY-del): a spinning top; a game played during Chanukah.

Elijah: custom has it to leave a cup of wine and a door open for the prophet Elijah during the Seder in the hope that he will return to earth.

Groggers: noisemakers used to blot out Haman's name during the reading of the Megillah on Purim.

Haggadah (Ha-GAH-da): Hebrew for "a telling." A special book read during the Seder that details the narration of the Passover story of the Jews' journey to freedom from slavery in Egypt.

Hamantaschen (HA-man-tash-en): triangle-shaped pastries named after the wicked Haman, eaten during Purim.

Haroset (HAR-o-set): sweet paste of chopped apples, nuts, and wine that symbolizes the mortar the Israelites used to build pyramids when they were slaves in Egypt.

Kiddush (Ki-DOOSH): the special blessing for Sabbath and holidays said over a cup of wine.

Kugel (KOO-gul): a noodle or potato pudding.

Latkes (LOT-kas): potato pancakes eaten during Chanukah.

L'shanah Tovah (Le-shah-NA-toe-va): Hebrew for "good year." A Happy New Year greeting.

Maccabee (MAC-a-bee): Hebrew for "hammer." The warriors who drove out King Antiochus's army and tried to make the Jews pray to their many gods instead of the One God they believed in.

Maḥzor (Makh-ZOR): a prayer book used during Rosh Hashanah and Yom Kippur.

Mandelbrot (MAHN-del-braht): dry, oblong-sliced almond cookies.

Matzoh (MAT-za): flat unleavened bread eaten during Passover.

Matzoh balls: round soup dumplings made from matzoh meal.

Megillah (MA-gill-a): Hebrew for "a scroll." The scroll of Esther read during Purim. (Queen Esther saved the Jews from destruction at the hands of the evil Haman, revealing his plot to the King.)

Menorah (Me-NO-rah): a nine-armed candelabrum; eight arms represent each night of the holiday, the ninth is the shammash that lights the other candles.

Passover: eight-day festival celebrating the Jews' exodus from Egypt. (Usually falls around the end of March or early in April.)

Purim (POOR-im): the holiday celebrating the end of Haman's plan to kill all the Jews of Persia. (Falls some time in February or March.)

Rabbi (RA-bye): ordained teacher of Jewish law authorized to decide questions of ritual; spiritual leader of the synagogue.

Rosh Hashanah (Rosh Hah-shah-NA): Hebrew for "head of the year." Rosh Hashanah and Yom Kippur are called the High Holy Days. Rosh Hashanah marks the beginning of the "Days of Awe," which end on Yom Kippur, the most solemn day of the year. (Falls in September or October.)

Rugelach (RUG-a-lach): a small rolled pastry filled with raisins, ground nuts, cinnamon, sugar, and raspberry jam.

Seder (SAY-dur): Hebrew for "order." This special meal occurs on the first two nights of Passover. (Many religious people also have a special meal on the last two nights of this eight-day celebration.)

Shalach Manot (SHA-lach MA-note): sweet gifts of food given to friends and the poor during Purim.

Shammash (SHA-mas): the slightly raised ninth arm of the menorah (or chanukiah: Hebrew for "servant") or helper candle that lights all the other eight candles.

Shofar (Show-FAR): hollowed ram's horn blown during the Rosh Hashanah service to announce the new year.

Strudel (STROO-dul): a thinly layered flaky, stuffed pastry roll.

Sukkah (SOO-ka): partially open hut built during Sukkot to remind the Jews of how the Israelites lived in the wilderness.

Sukkot (Soo-COAT): Feast of Tabernacles, eight-day festival (falls between September and October) commemorating the final gathering of the harvest; a thanksgiving.

Synagogue (SIN-a-gog): Jewish house of prayer, also called a temple, or shul.

Tashlikh (Tash-LEEKH): ritual in which bread crumbs are tossed into a flowing body of water, symbolizing the casting away of sins to start a new year afresh during Rosh Hashanah.

Ten Plagues: the ten plagues visited on the Egyptians: Blood, Frogs, Lice, Beasts, Cattle Disease, Boils, Hail, Locusts, Darkness, Death of First Born. As part of the Passover Seder, the list is recited by everyone around the table, and a drop of wine is put on each person's plate as a plague is mentioned.

Zaide (ZAY-da): Yiddish for "grandfather."